This Book Belongs To

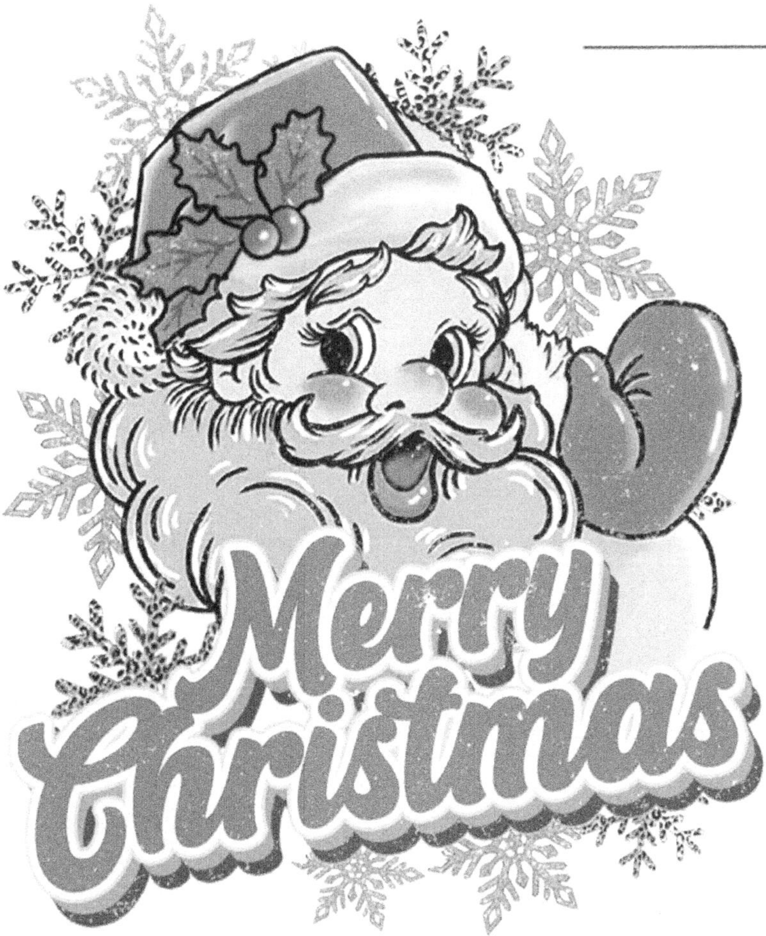

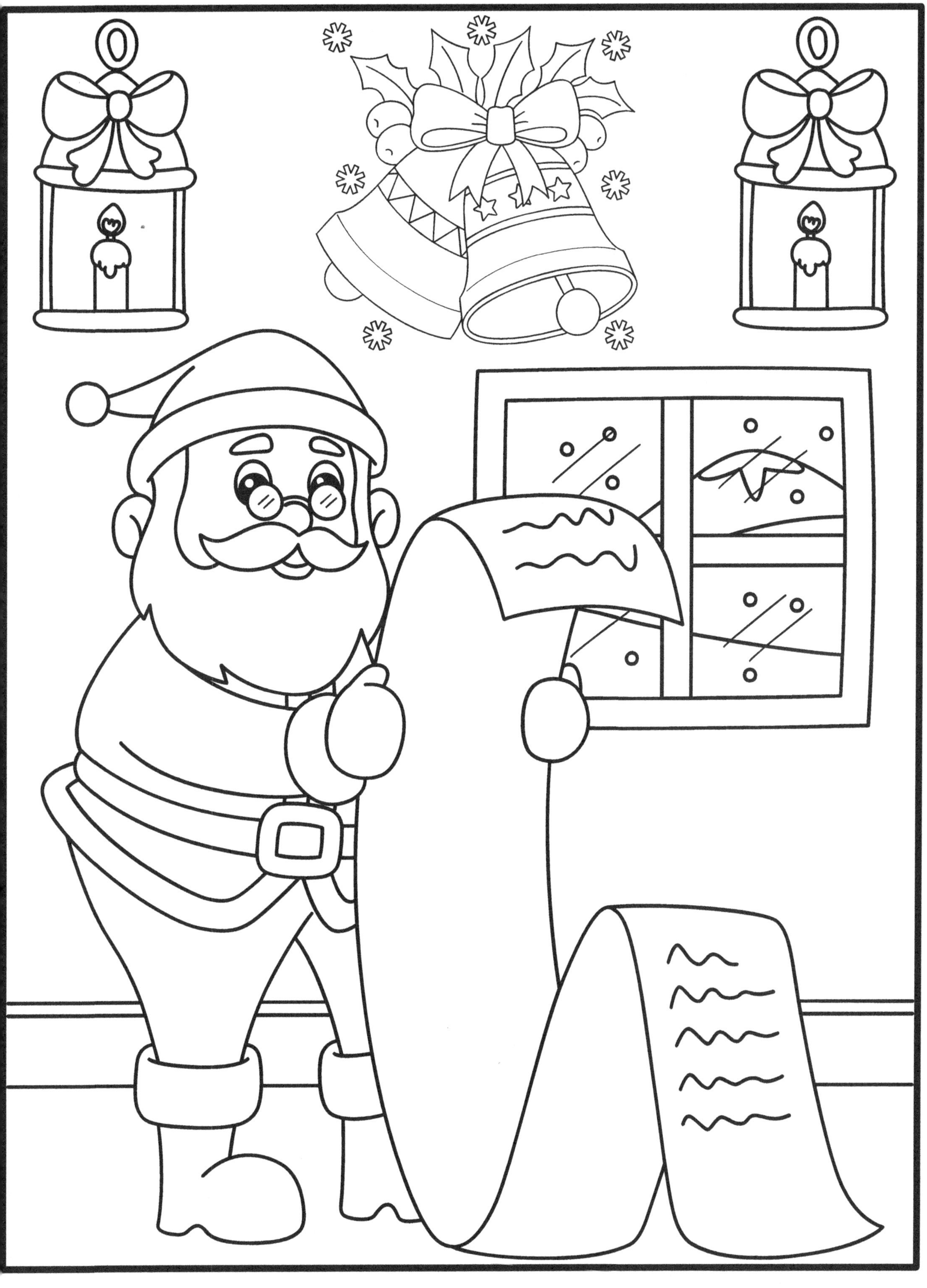

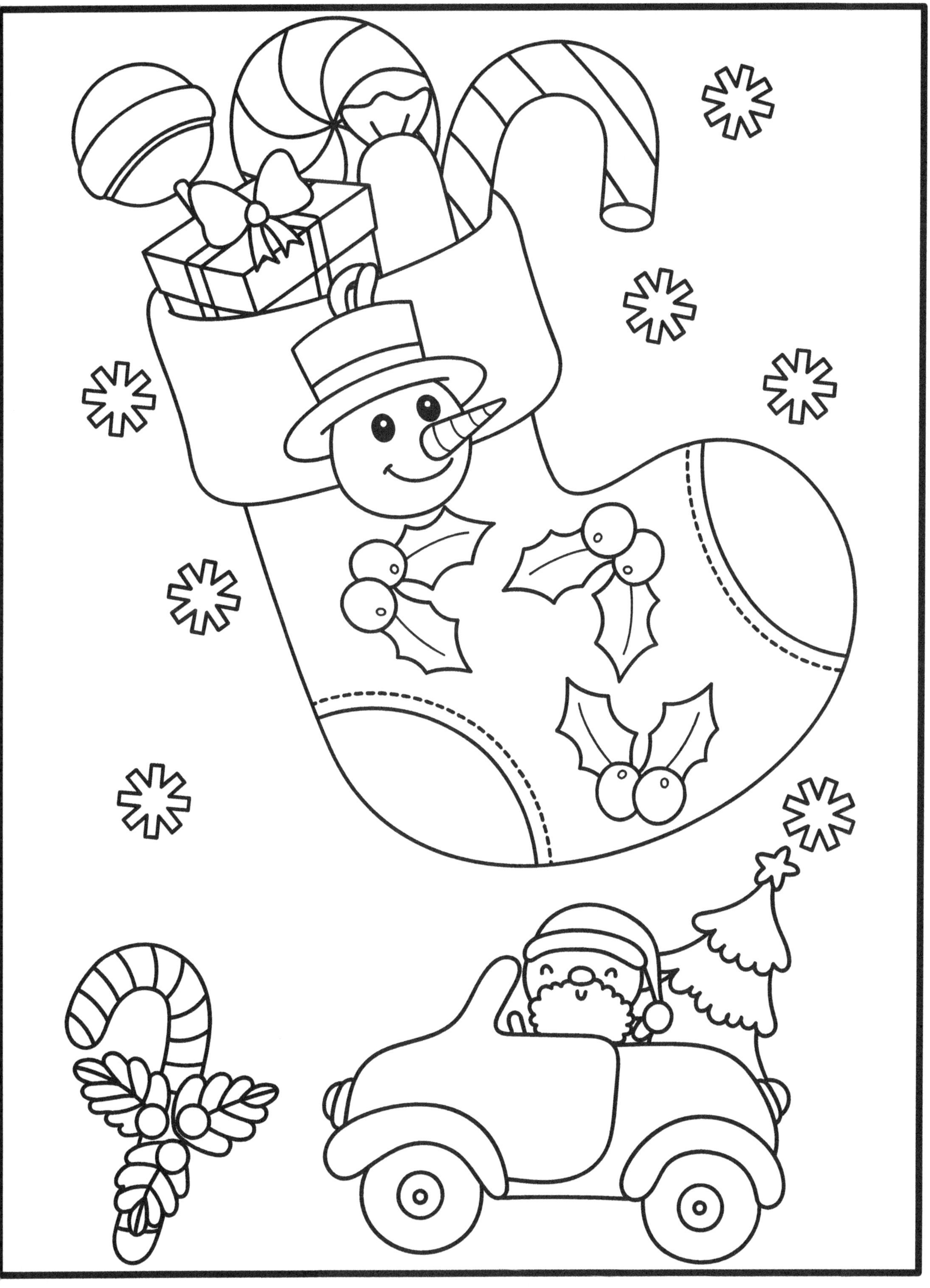

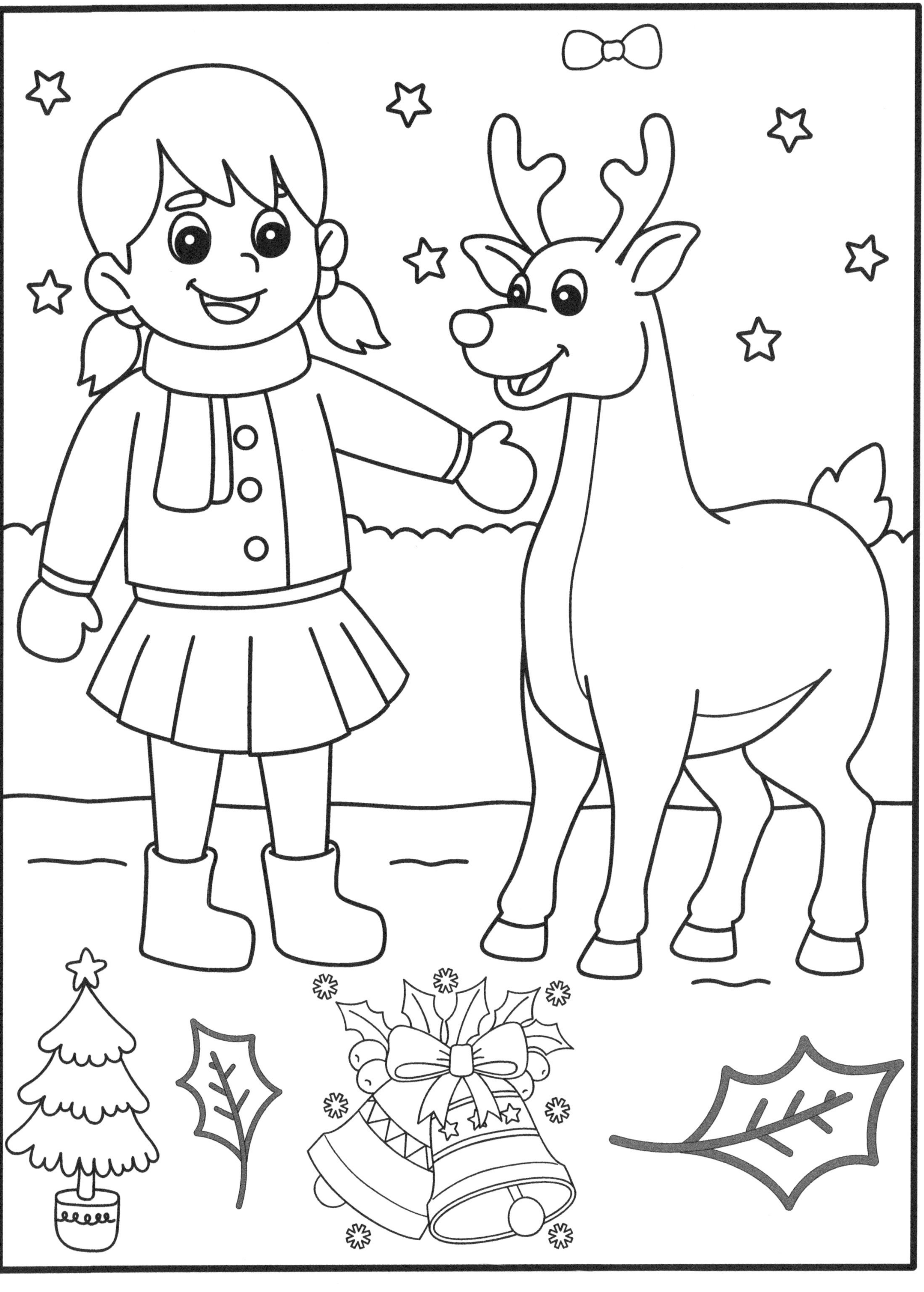

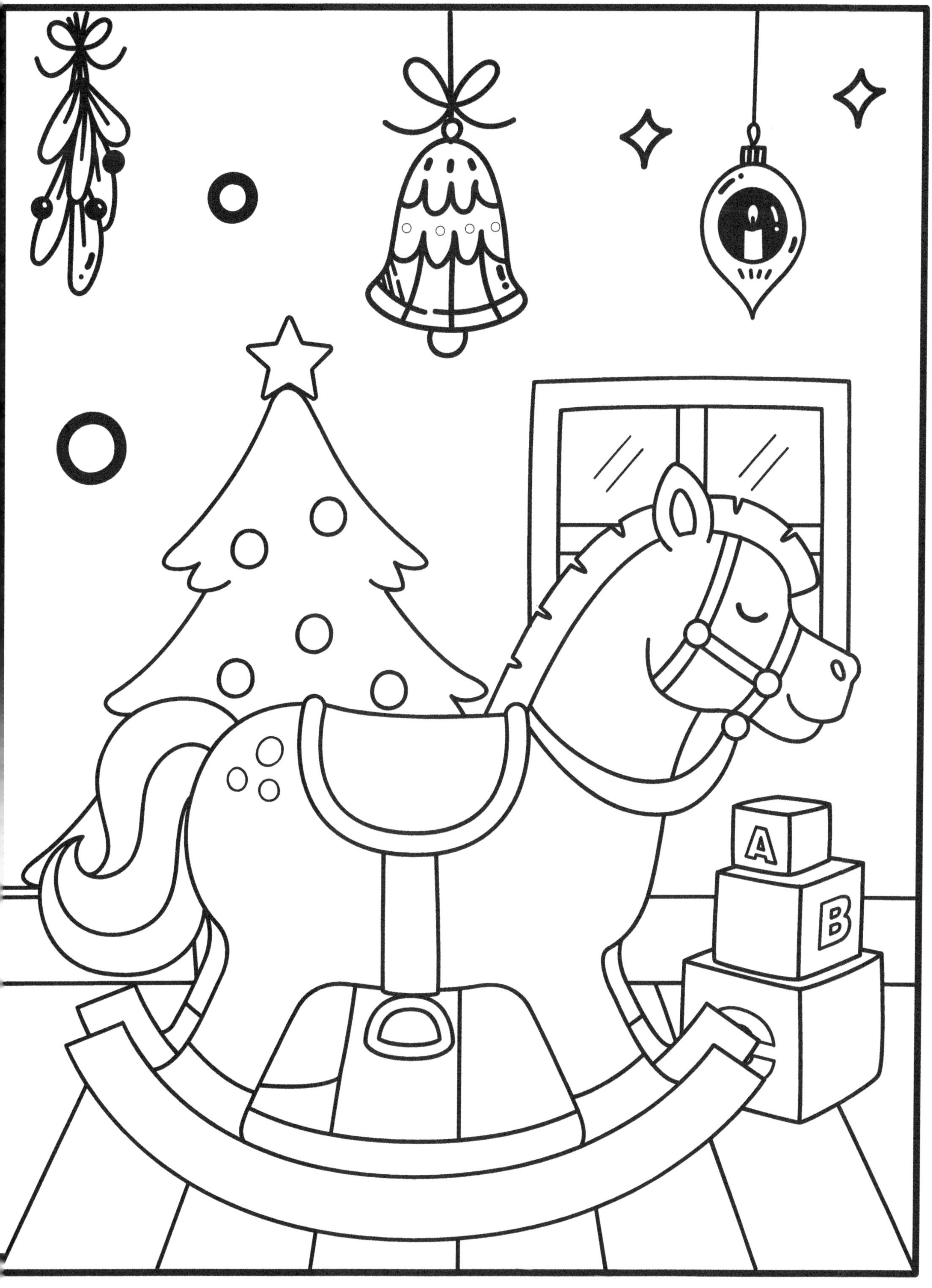
A
B

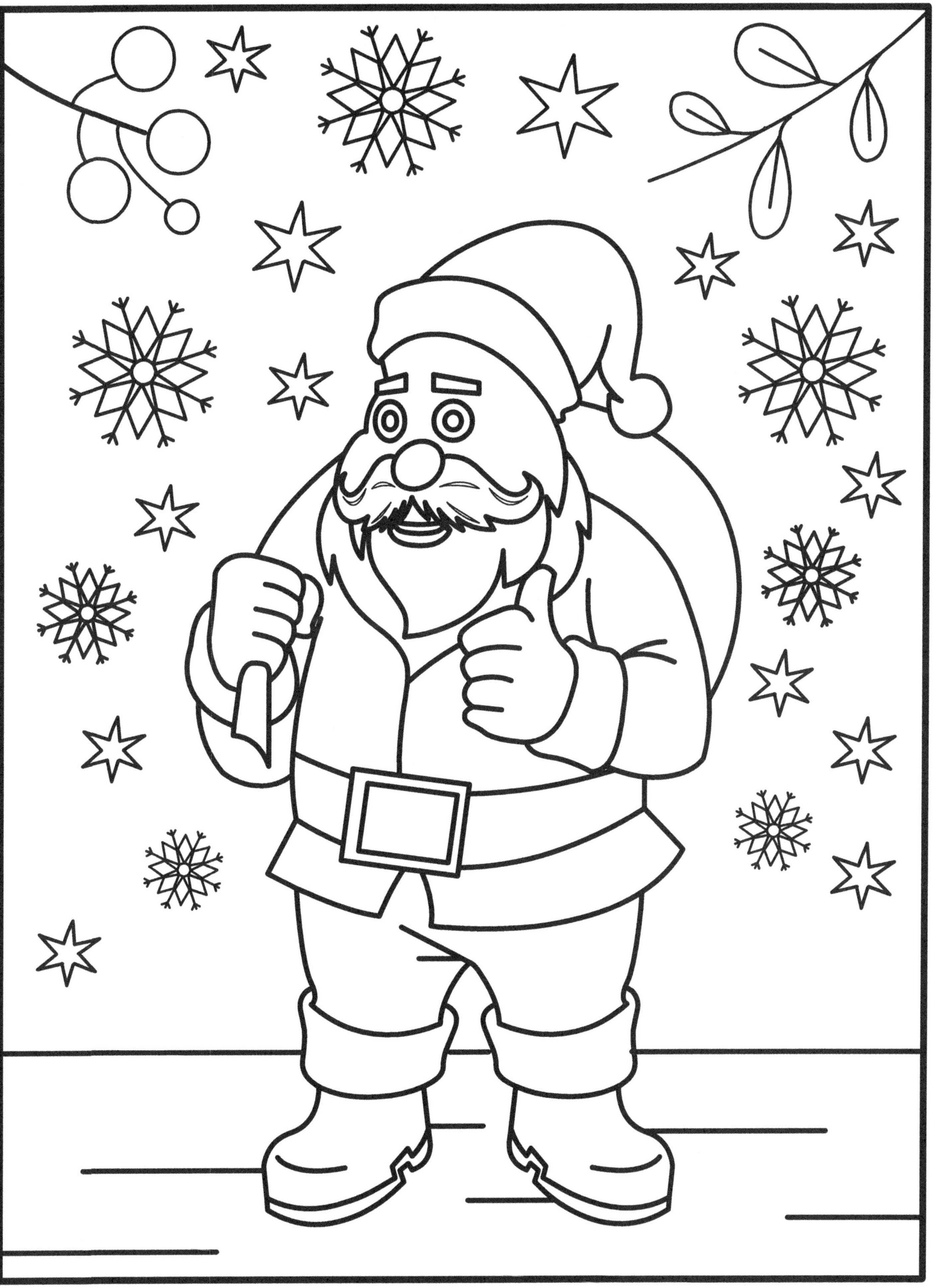

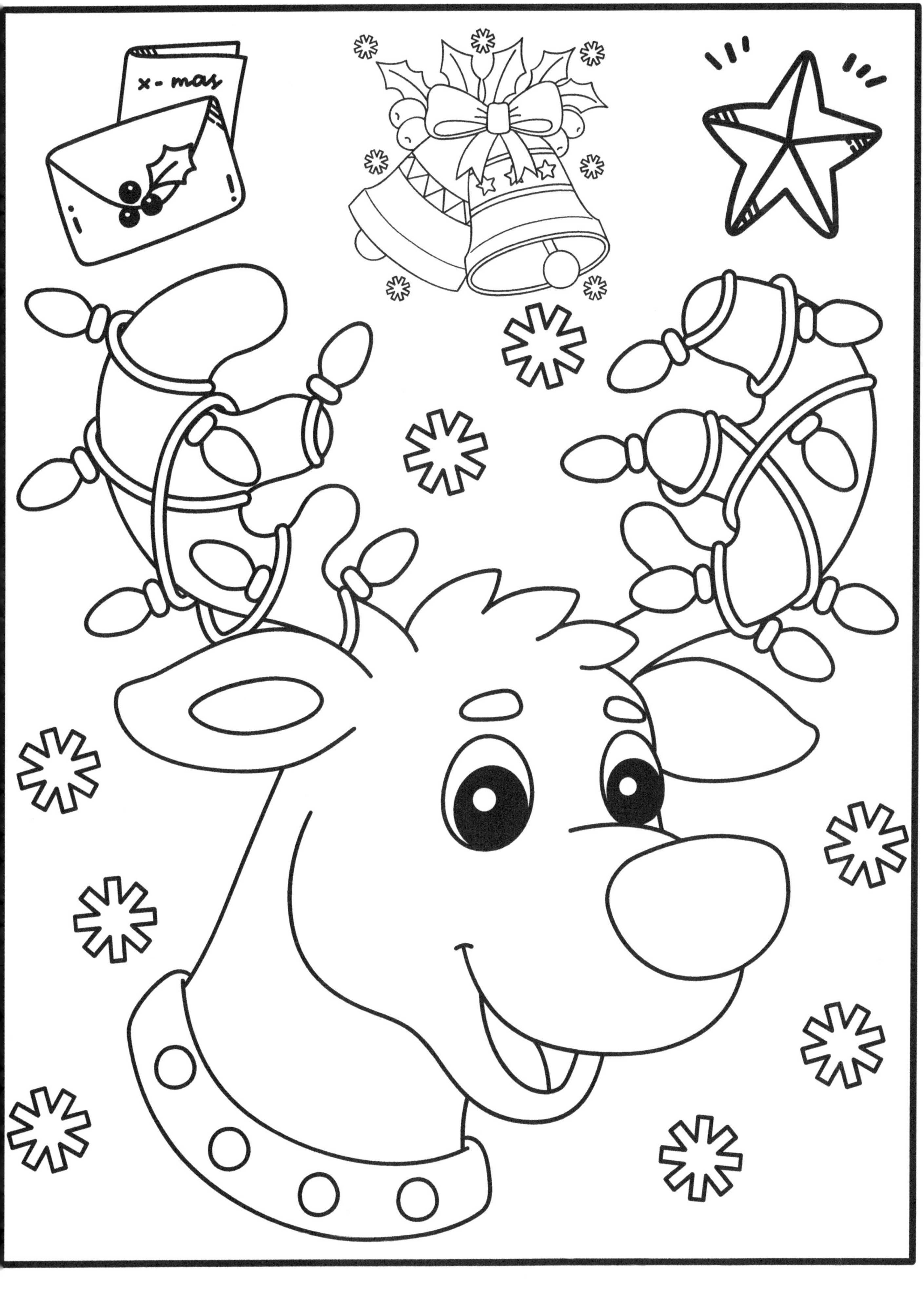
x-mas

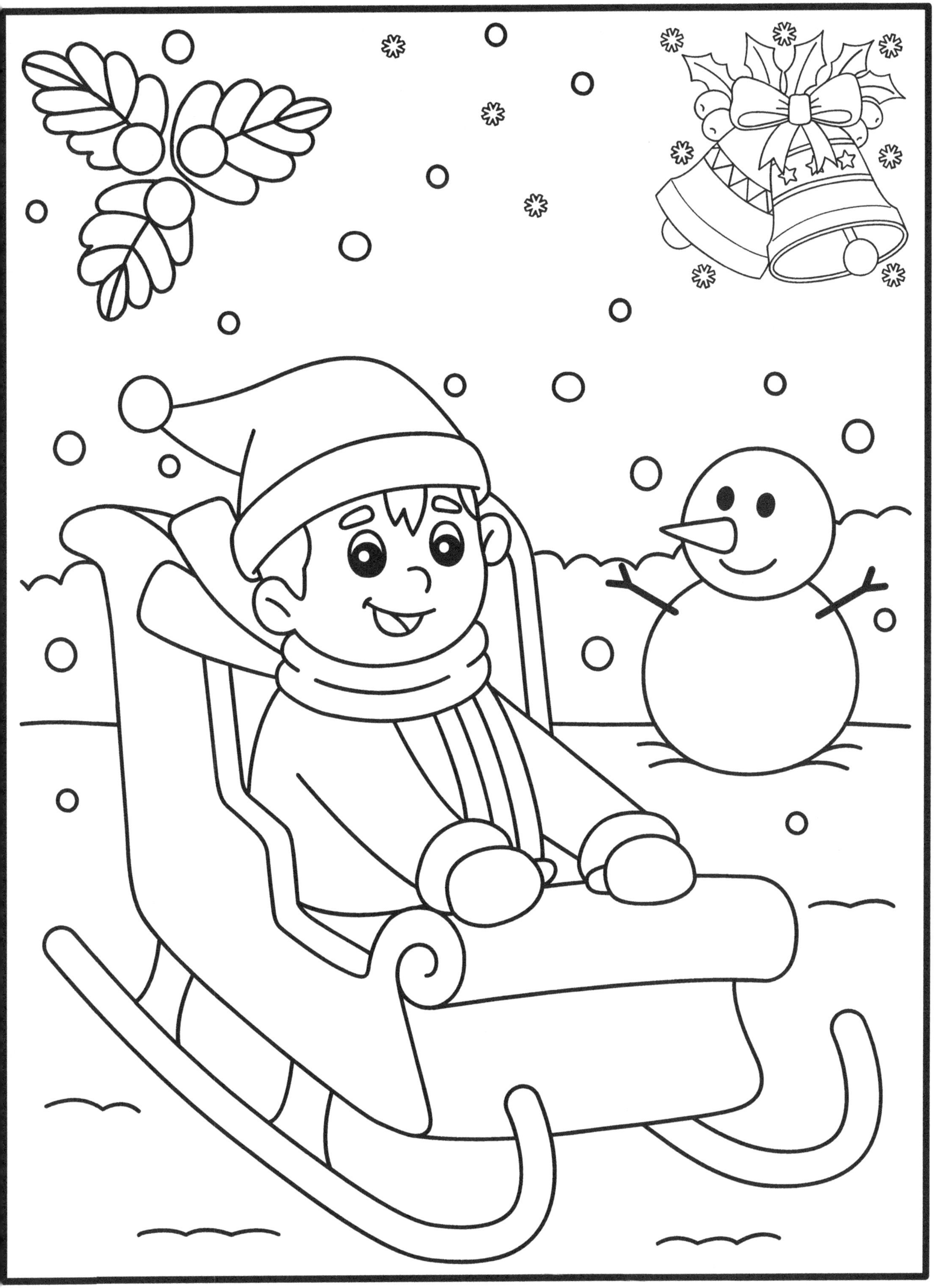

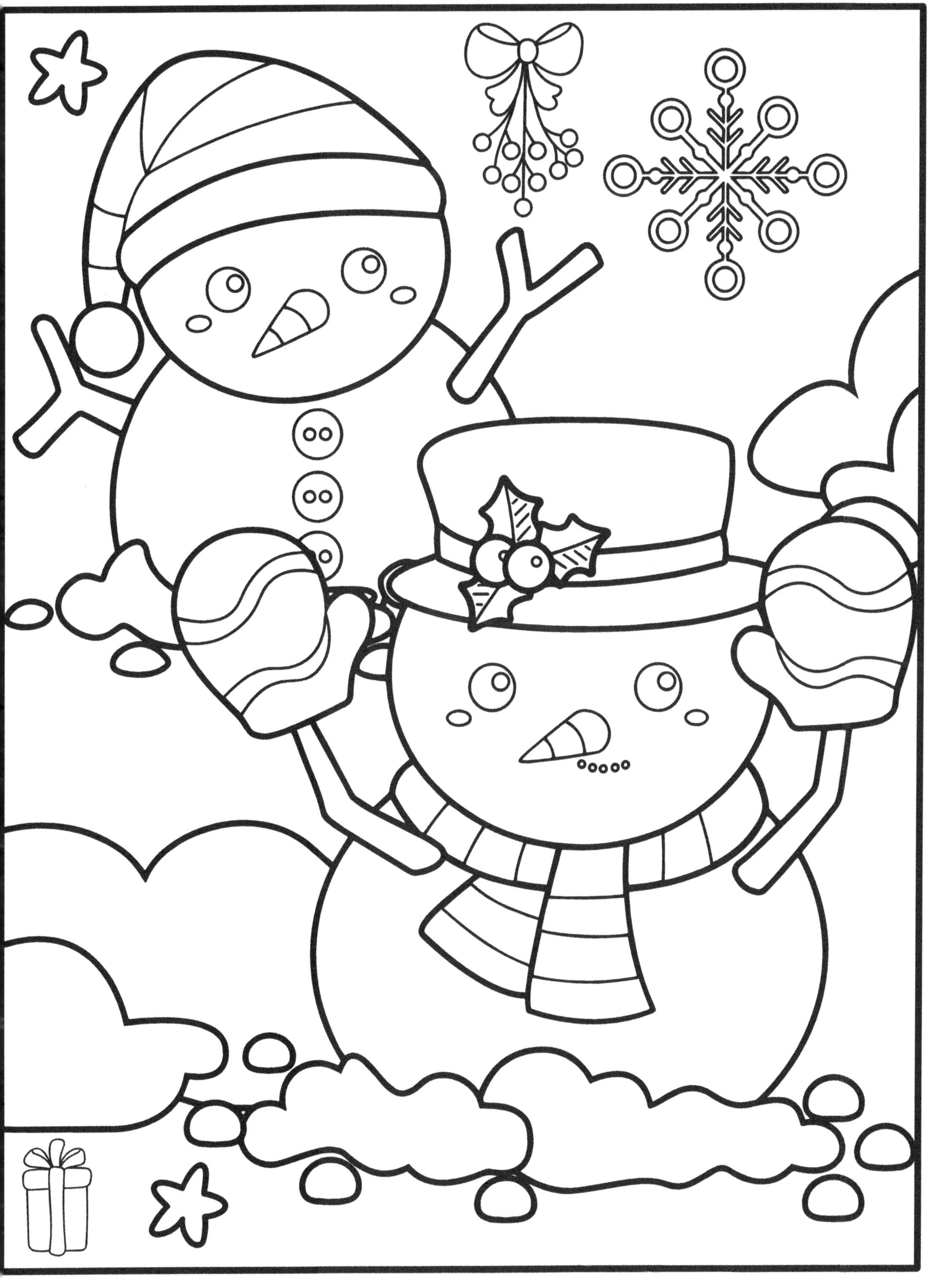

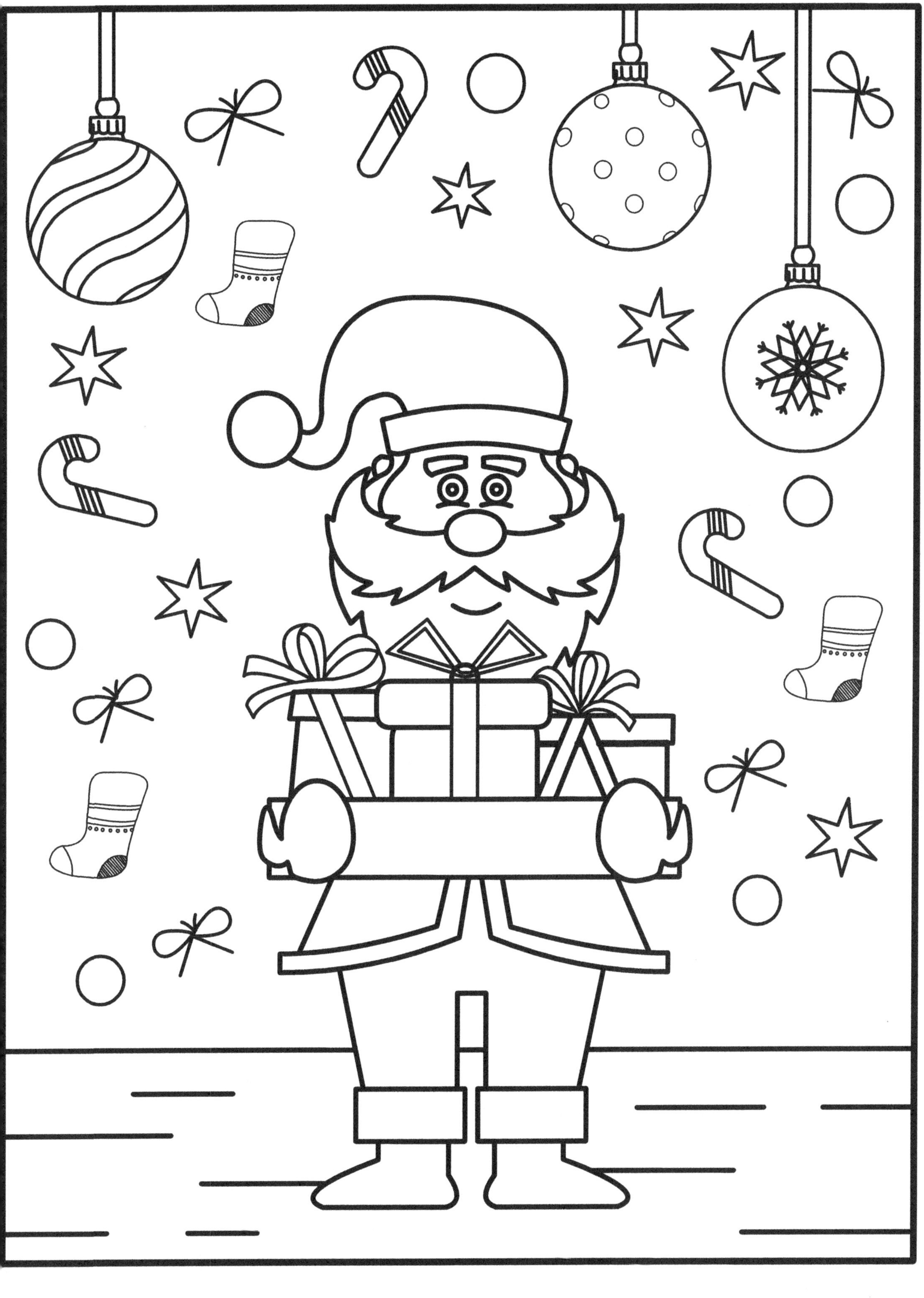

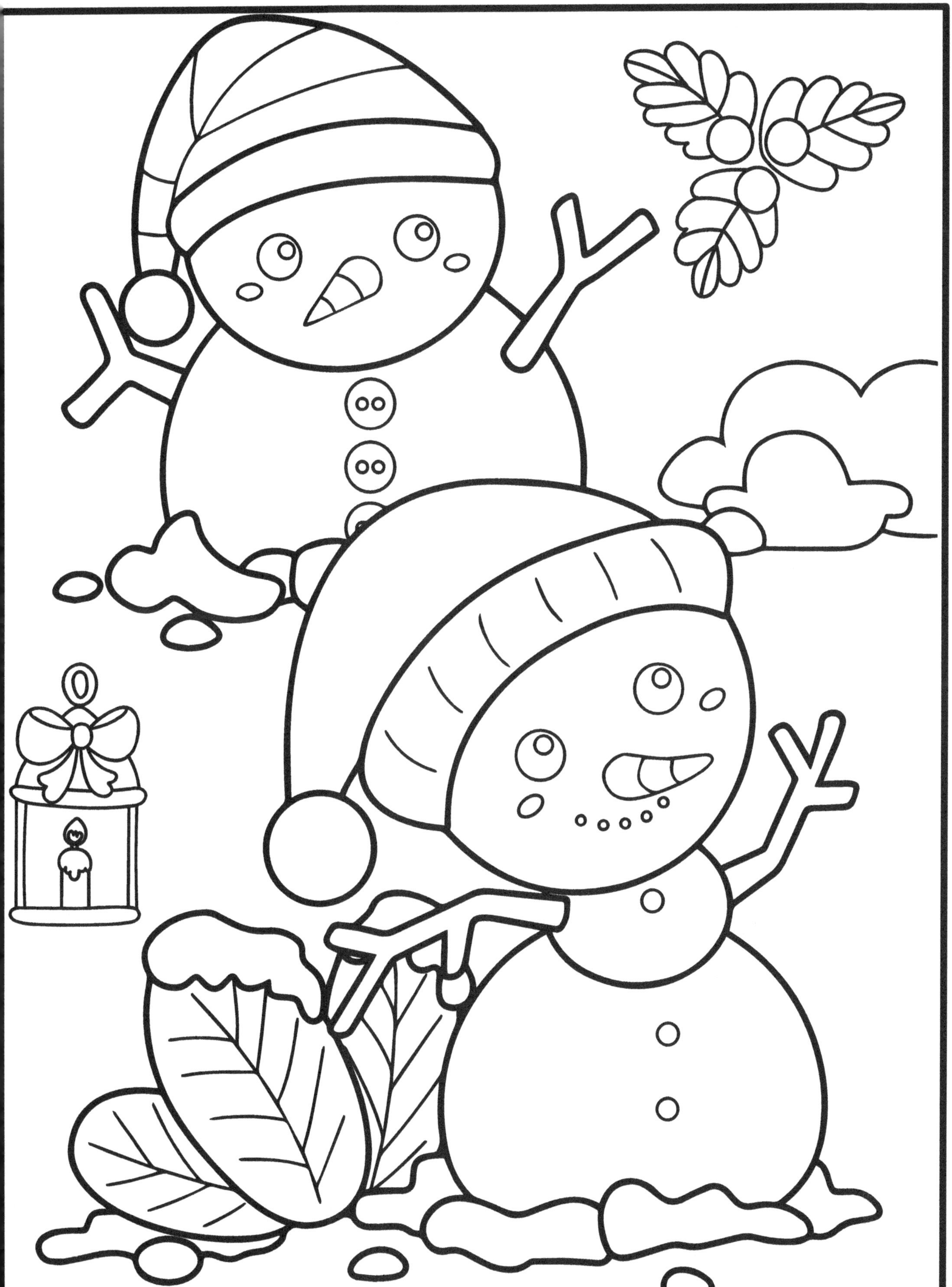

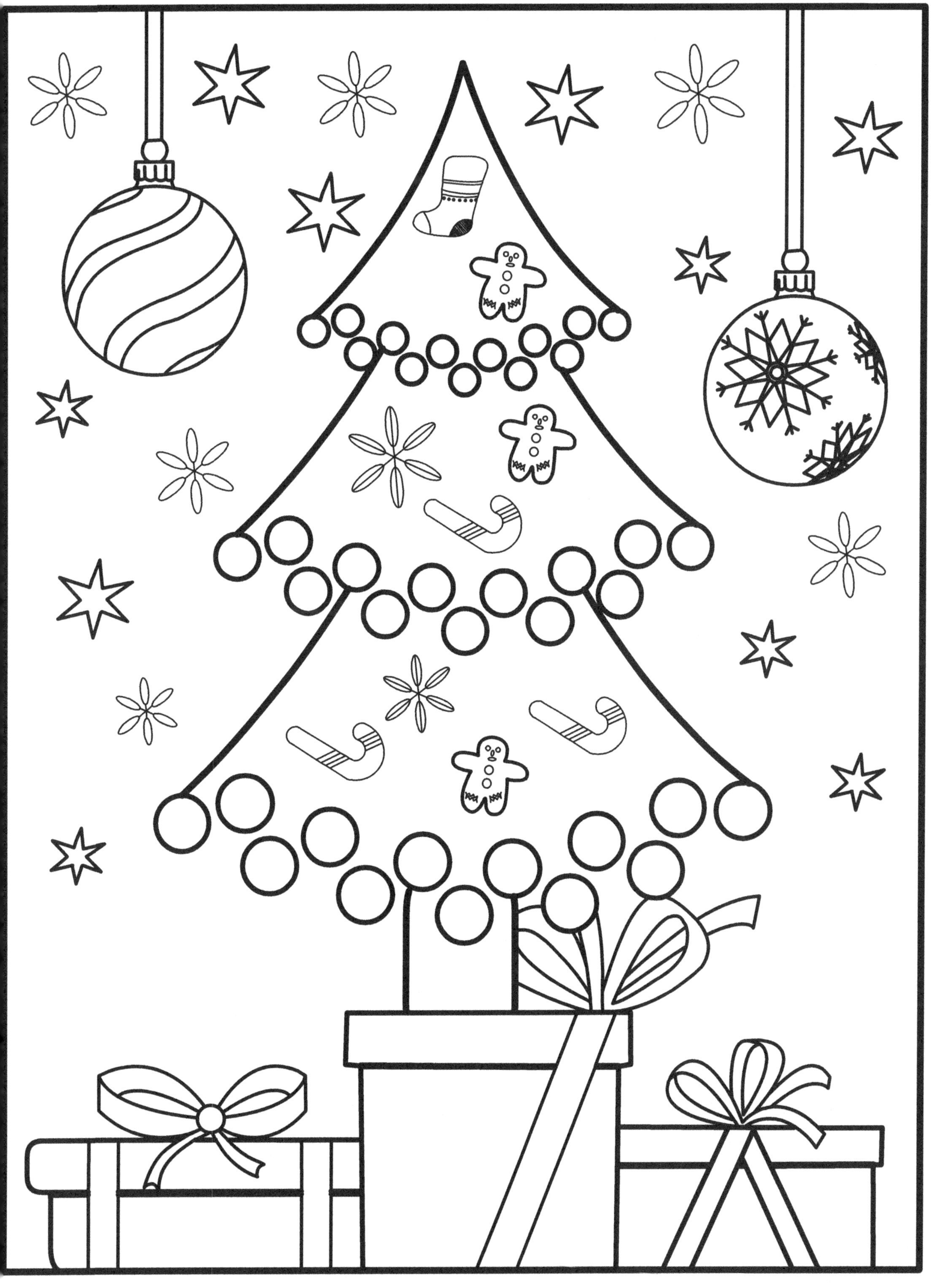

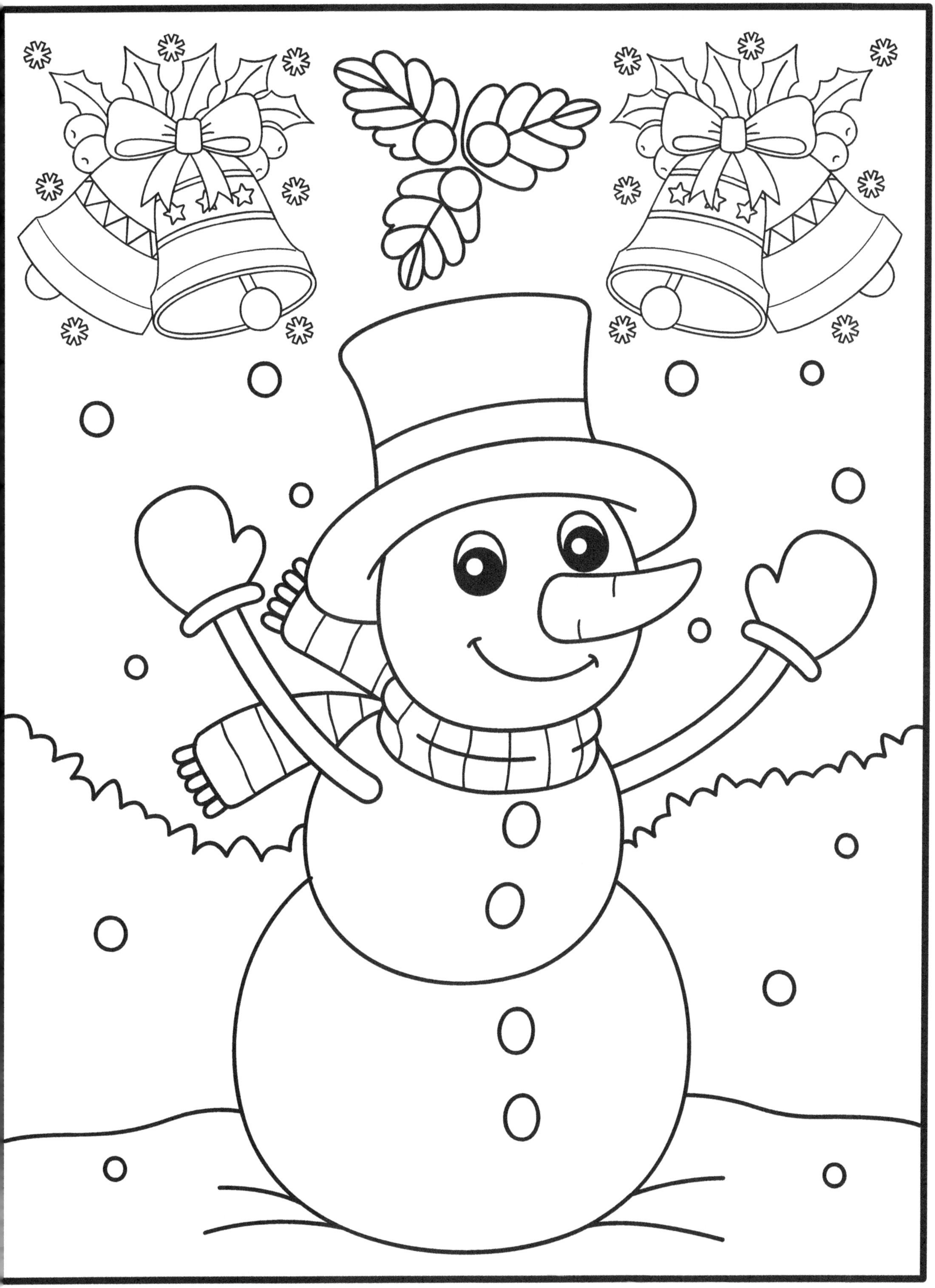

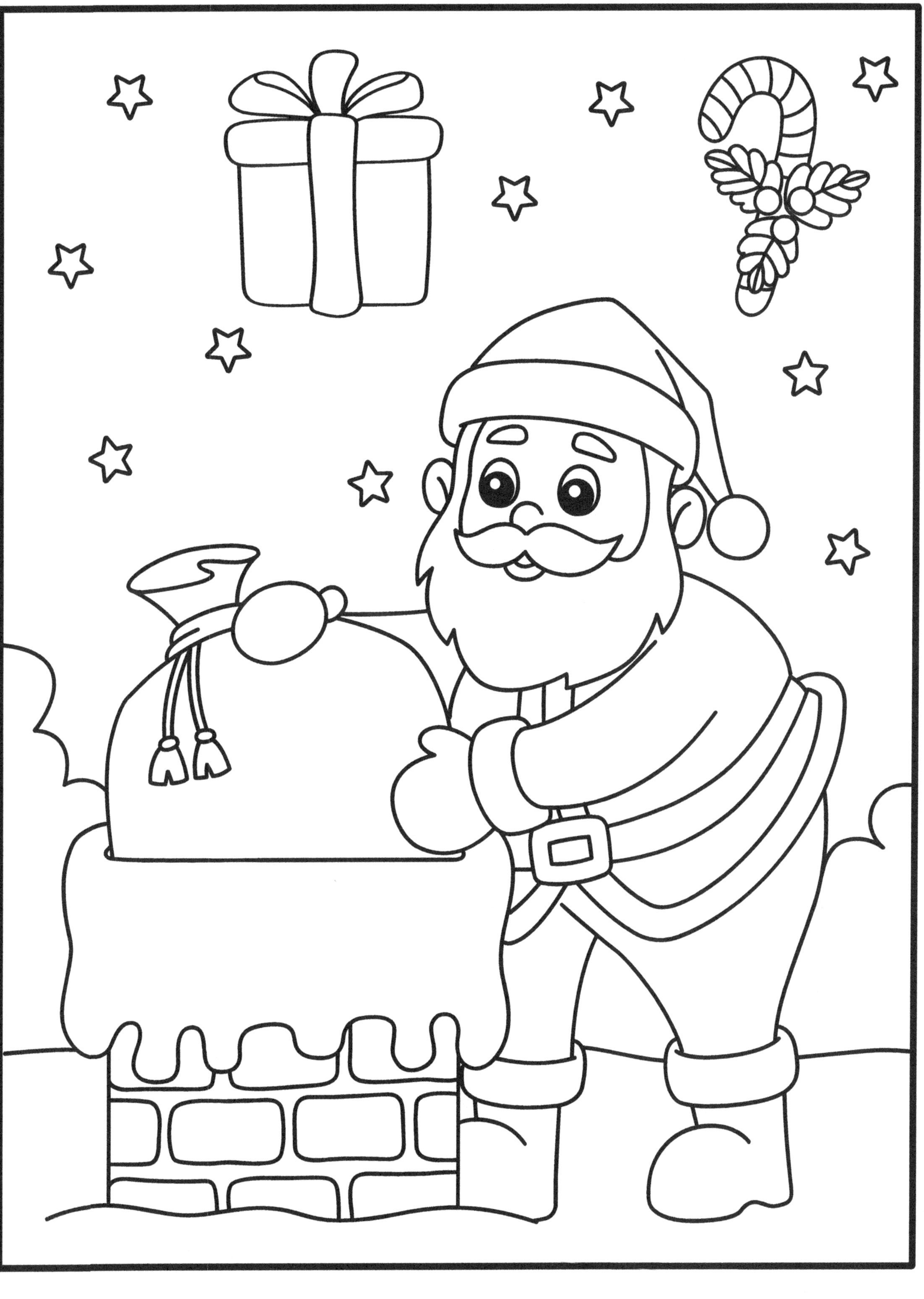

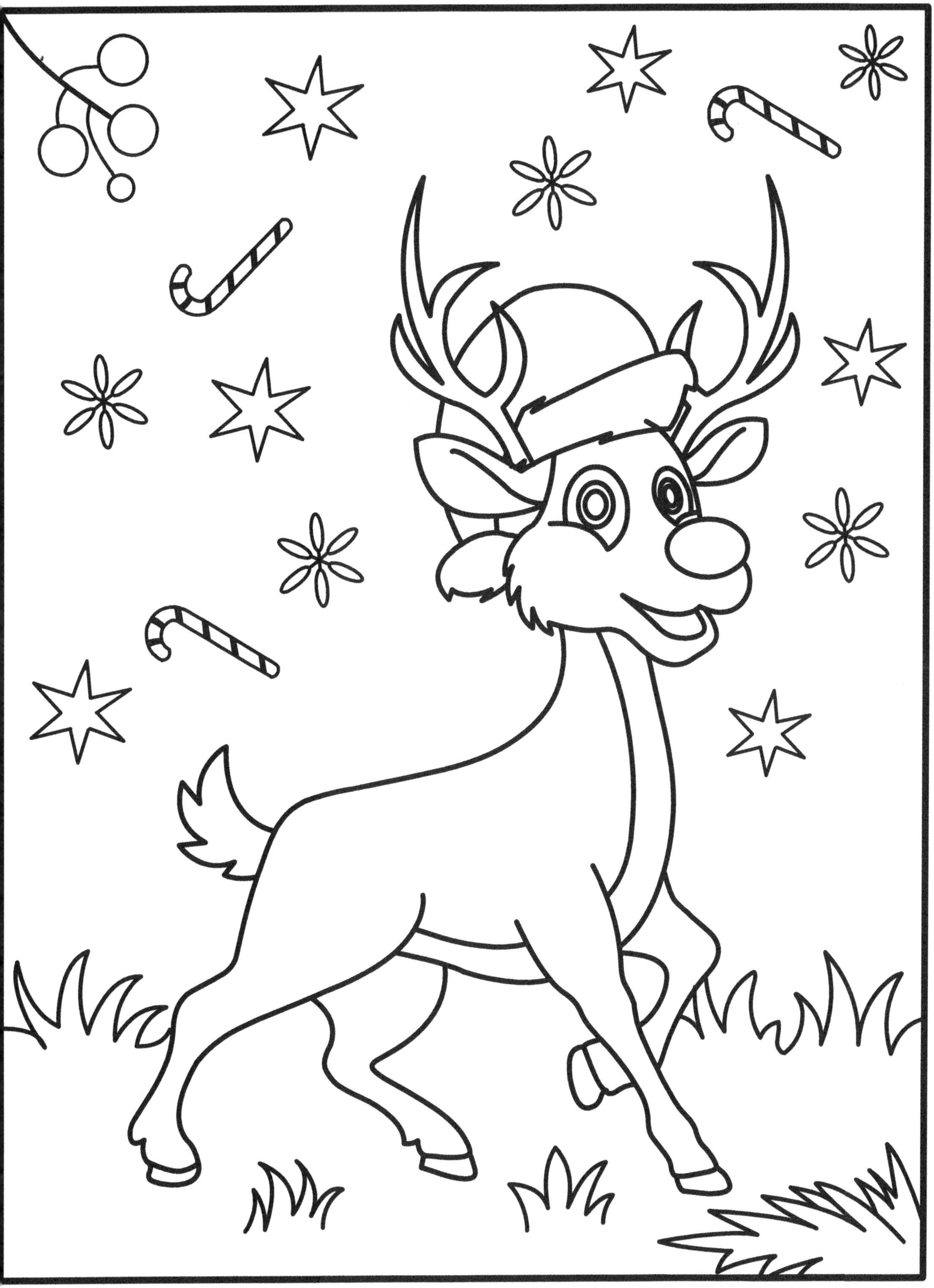

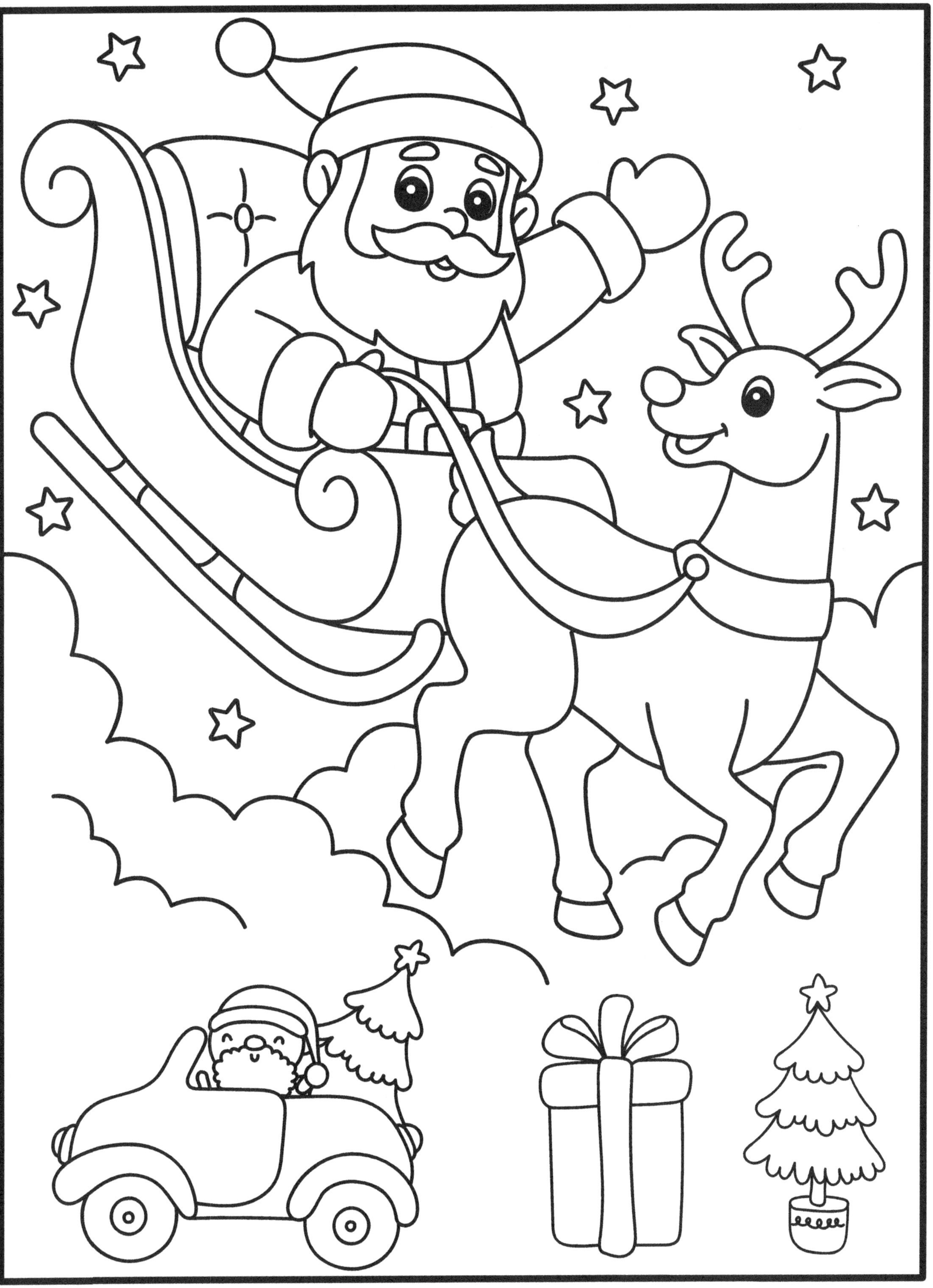

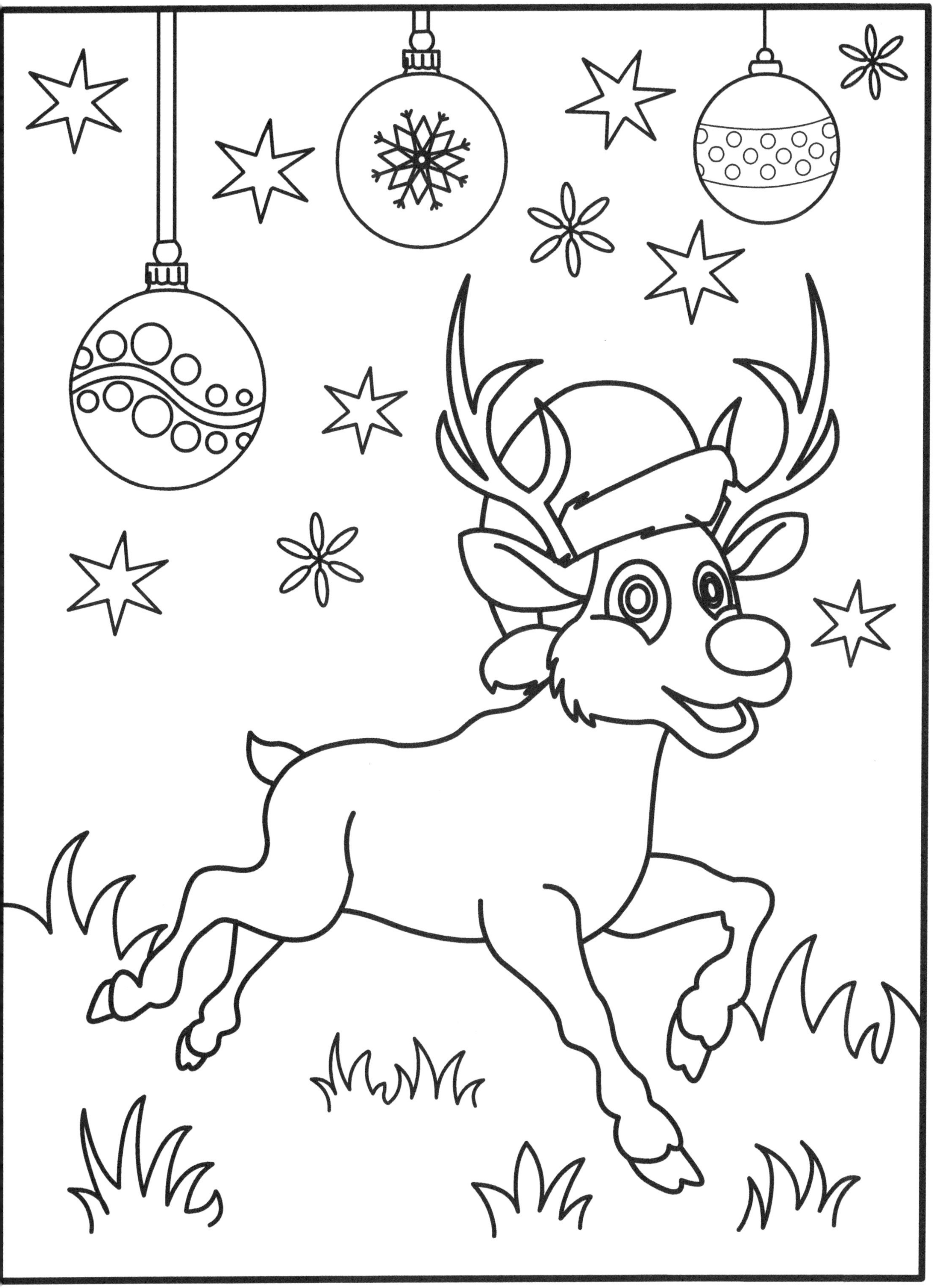

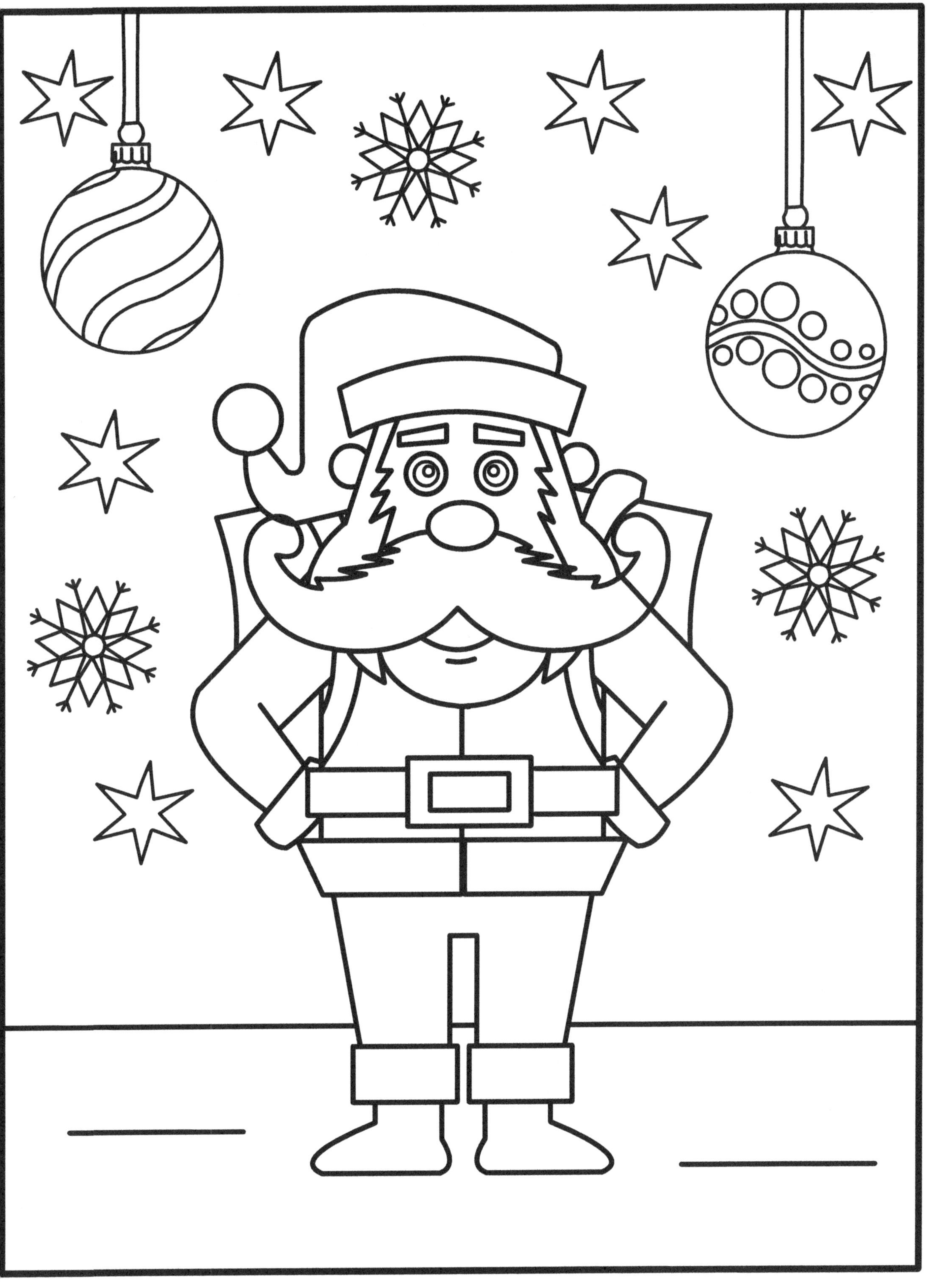

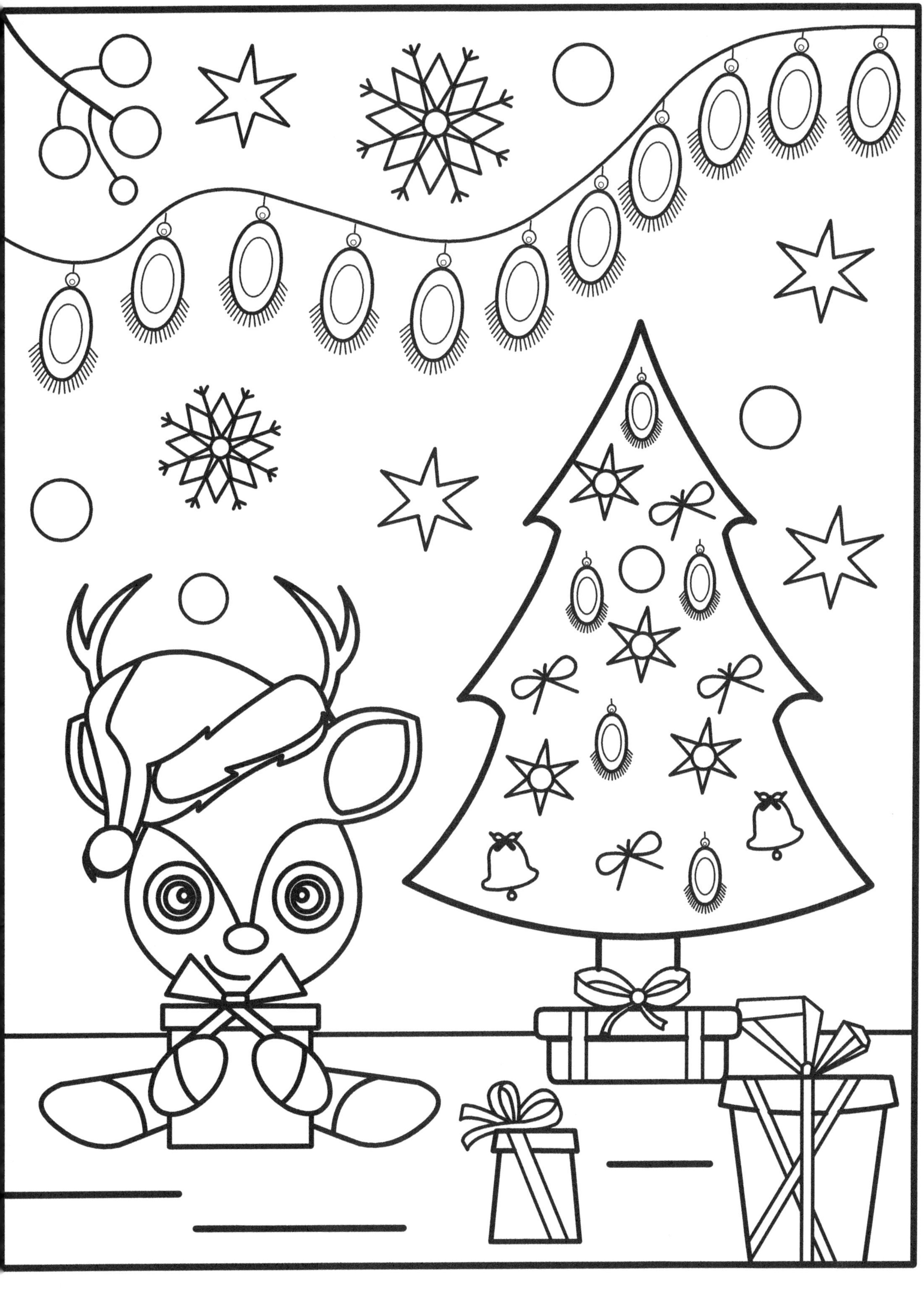

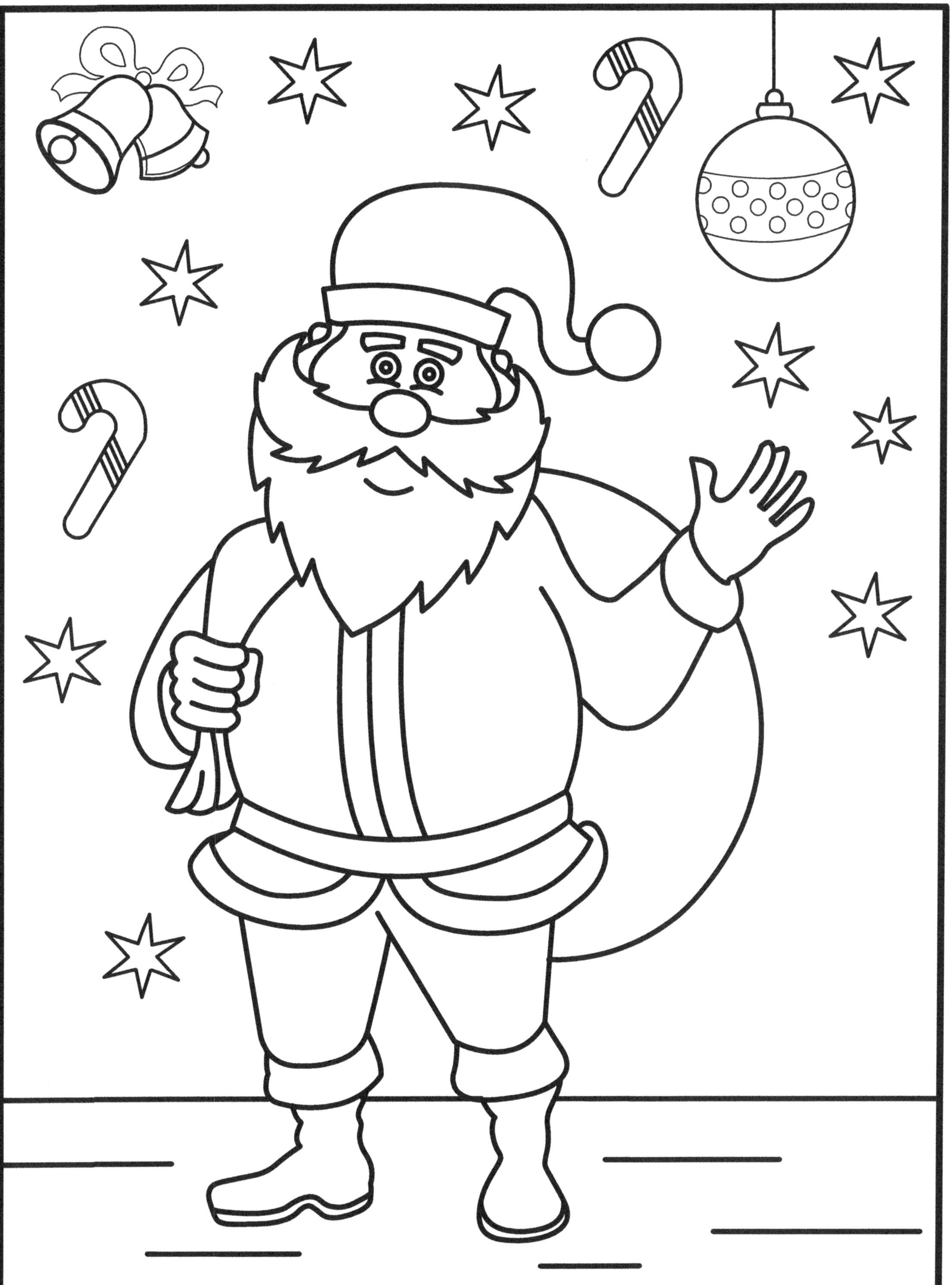

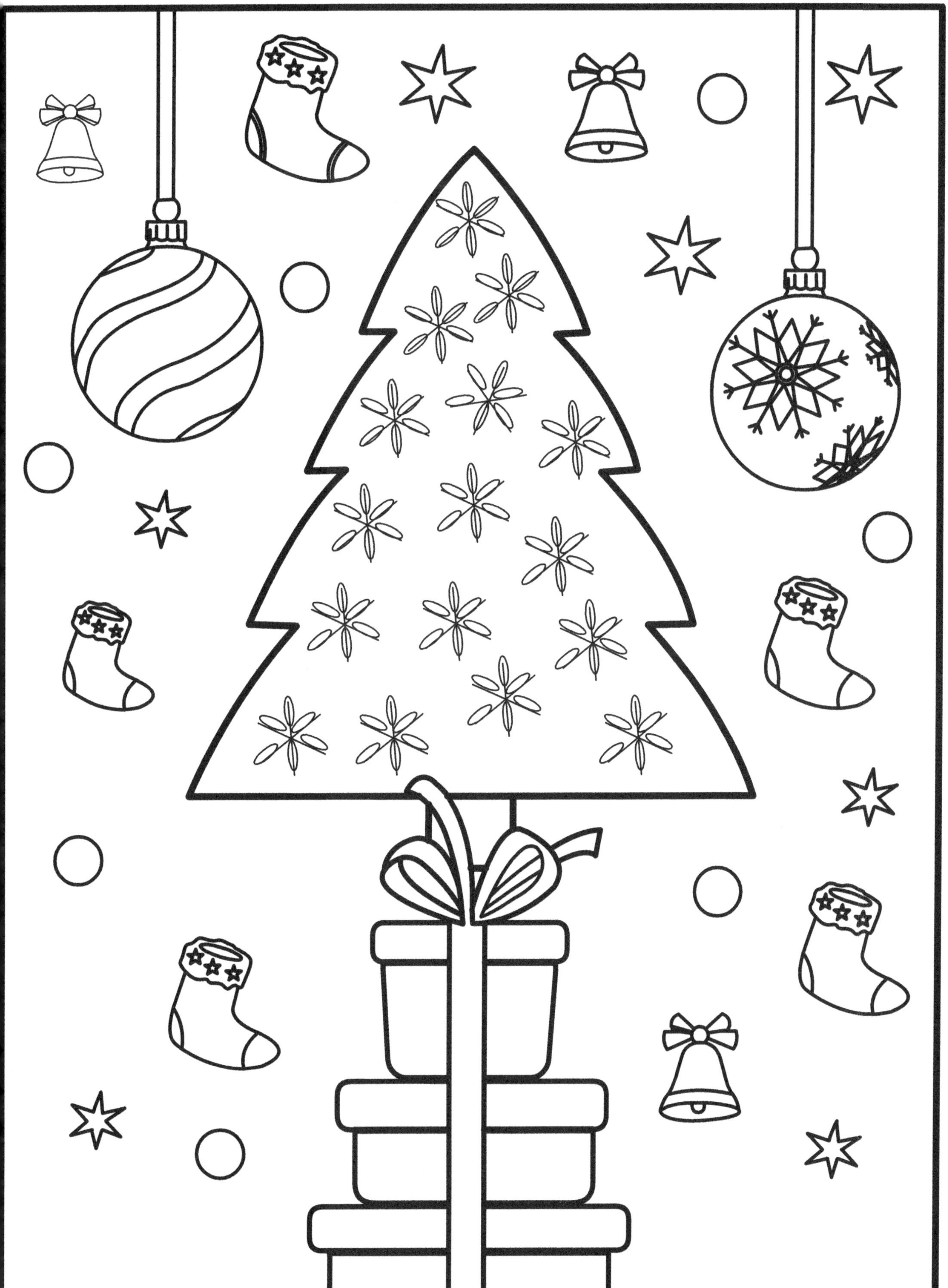

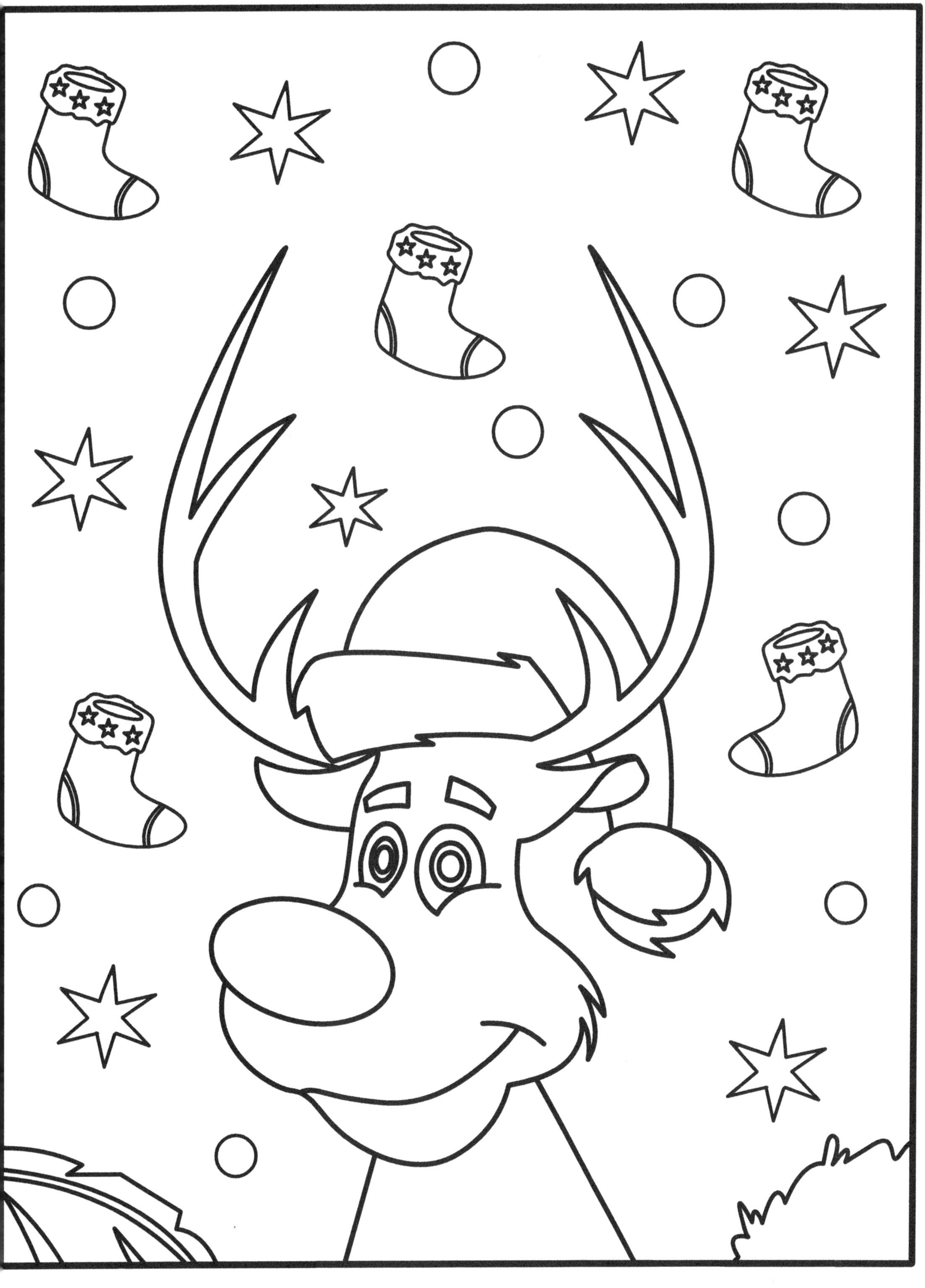

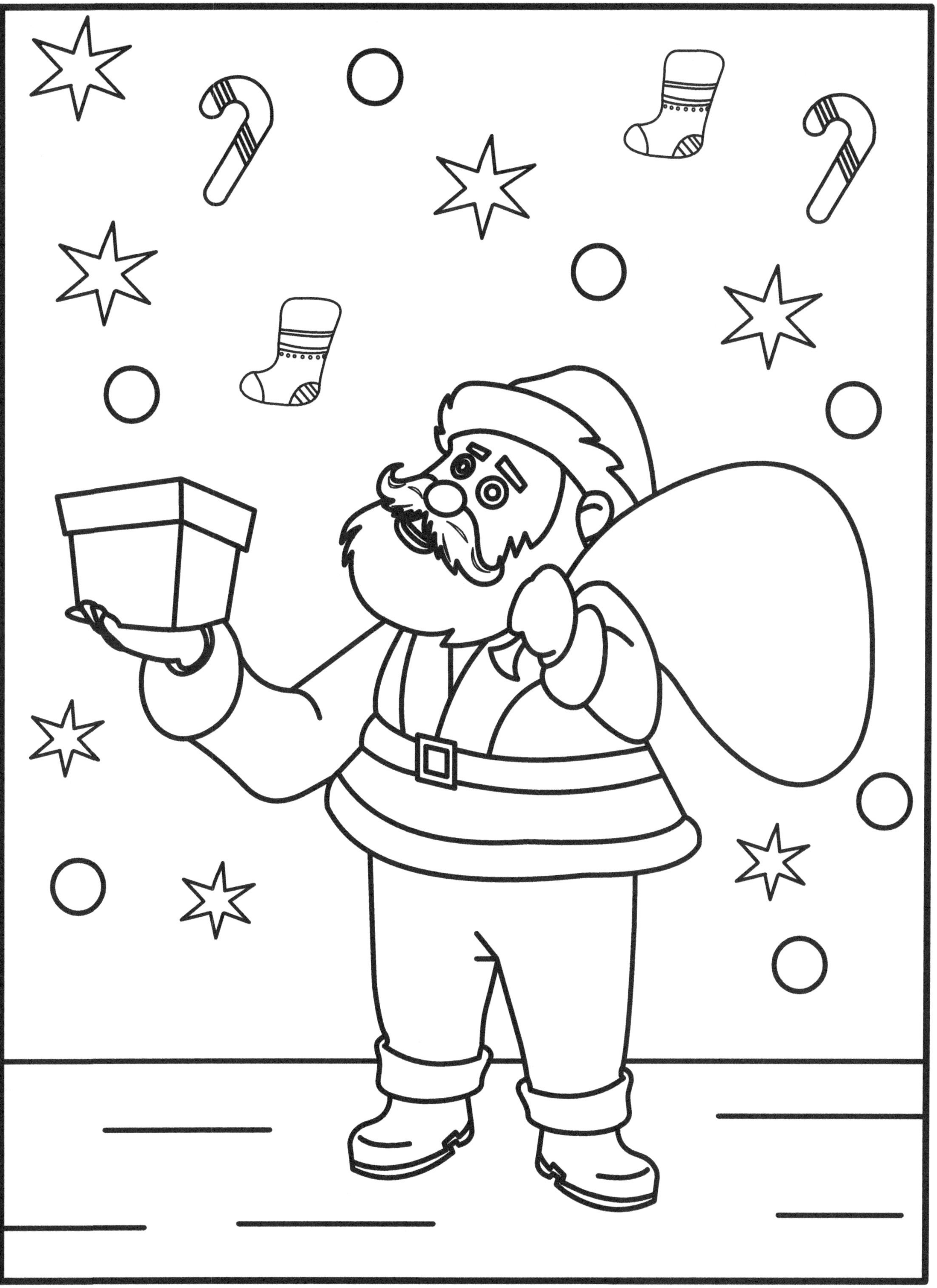

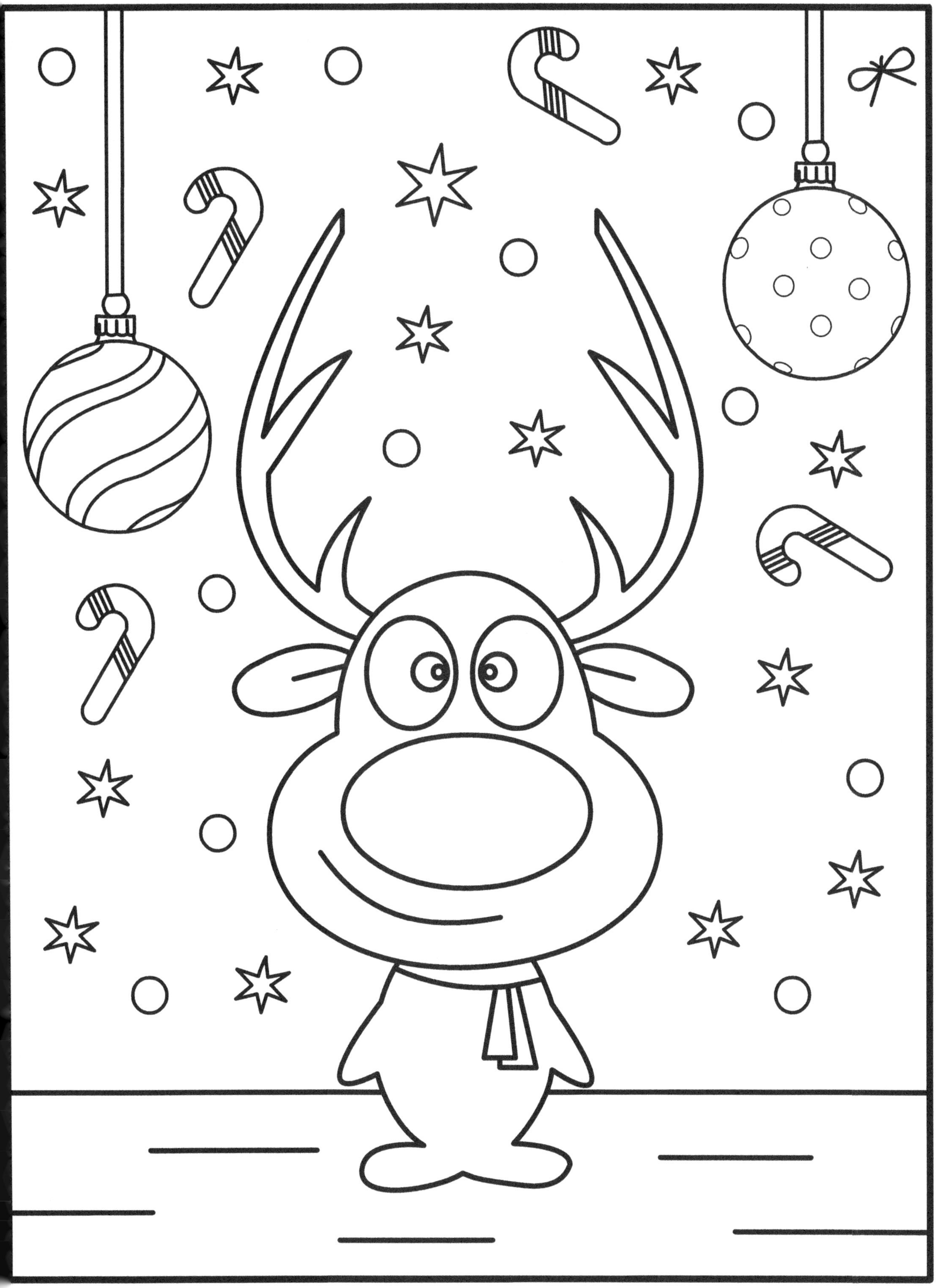

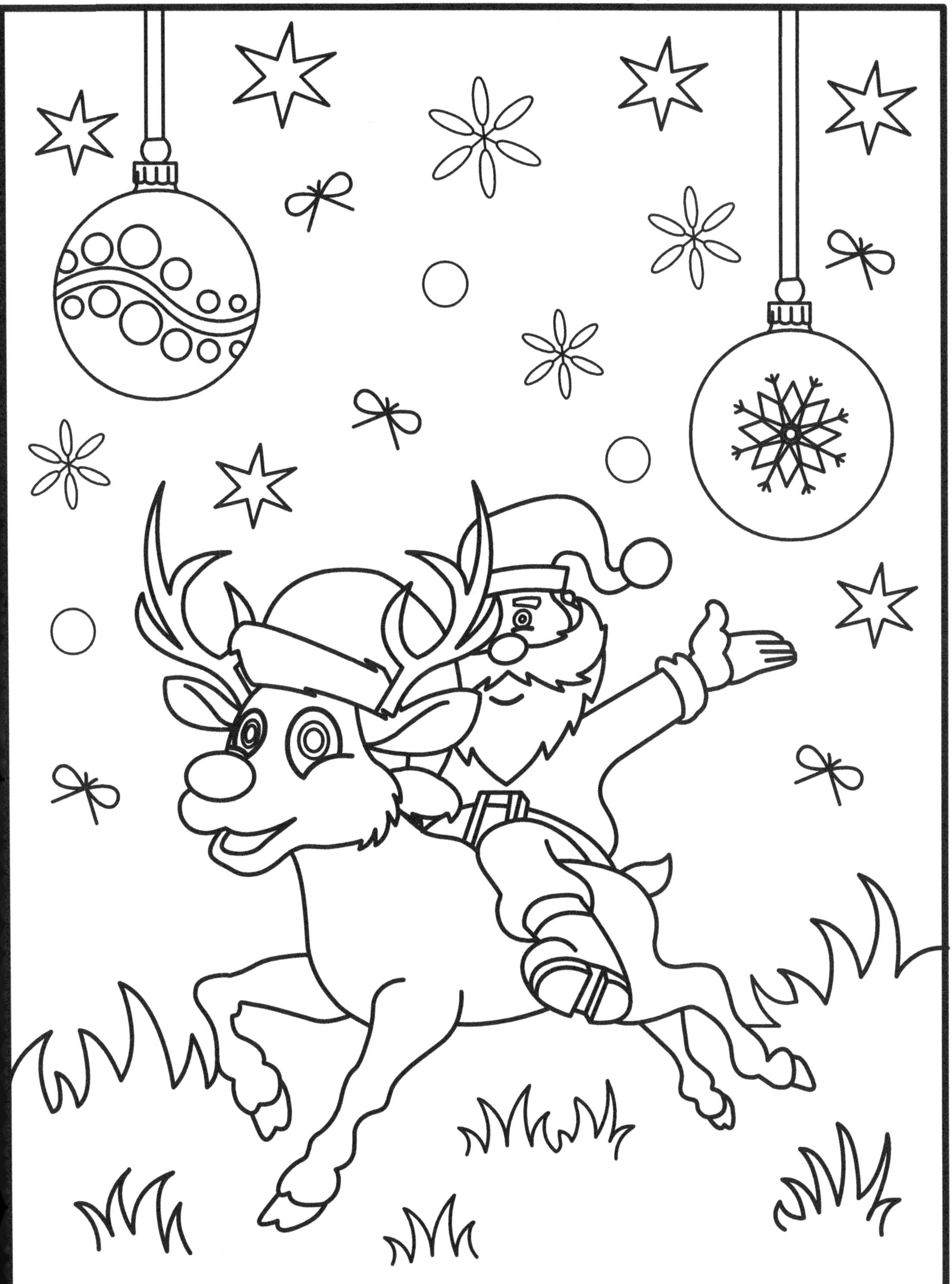

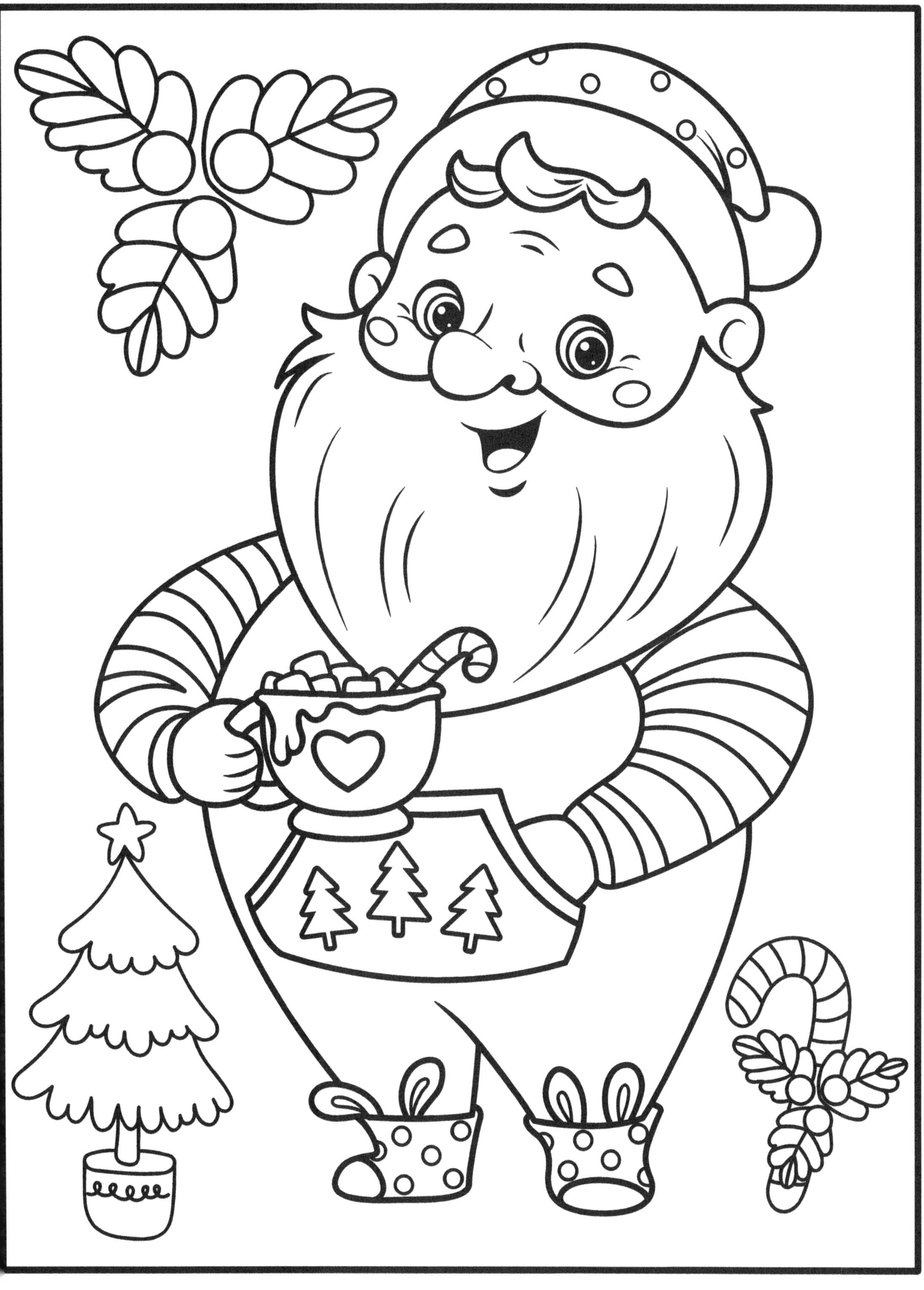

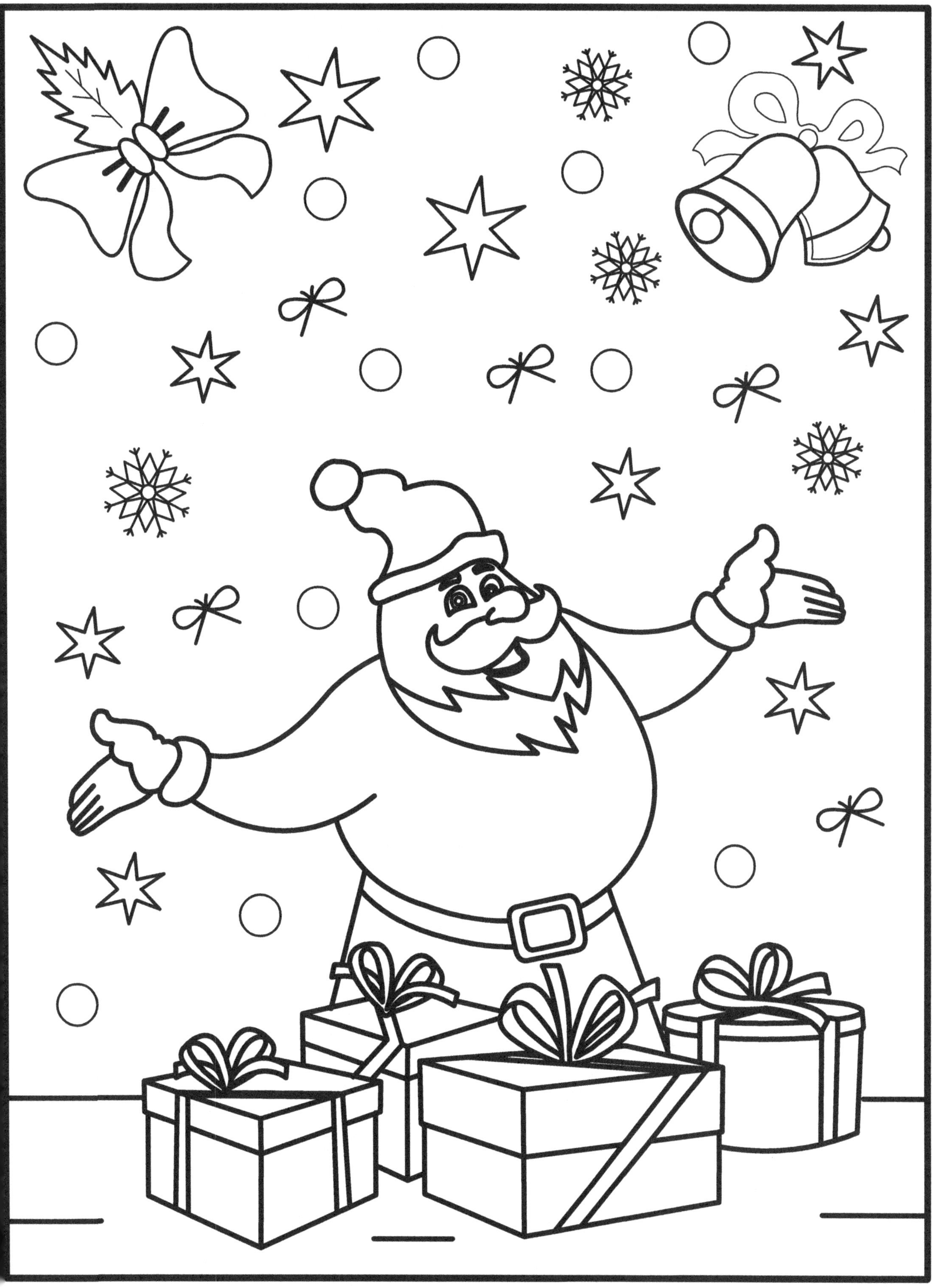

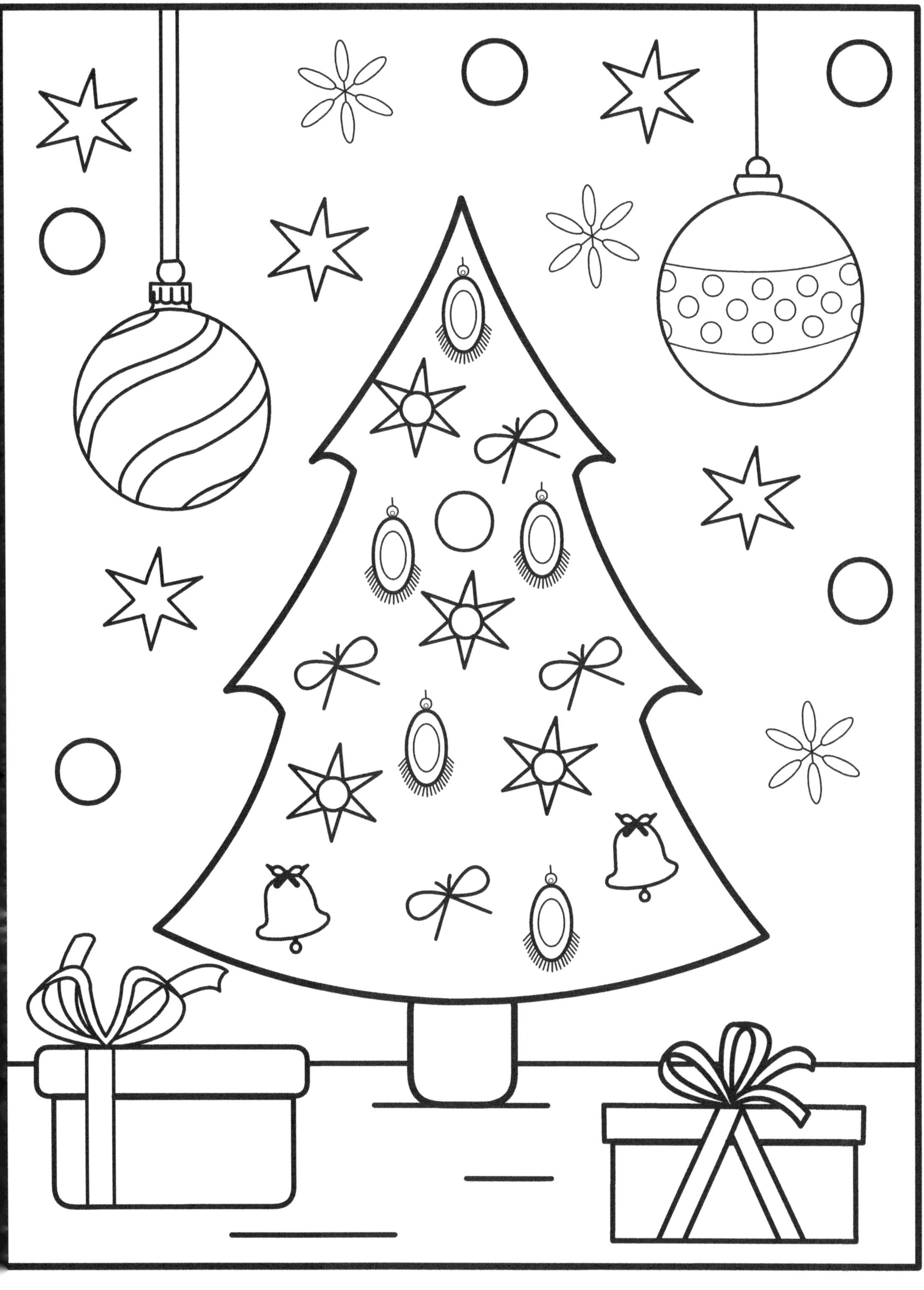

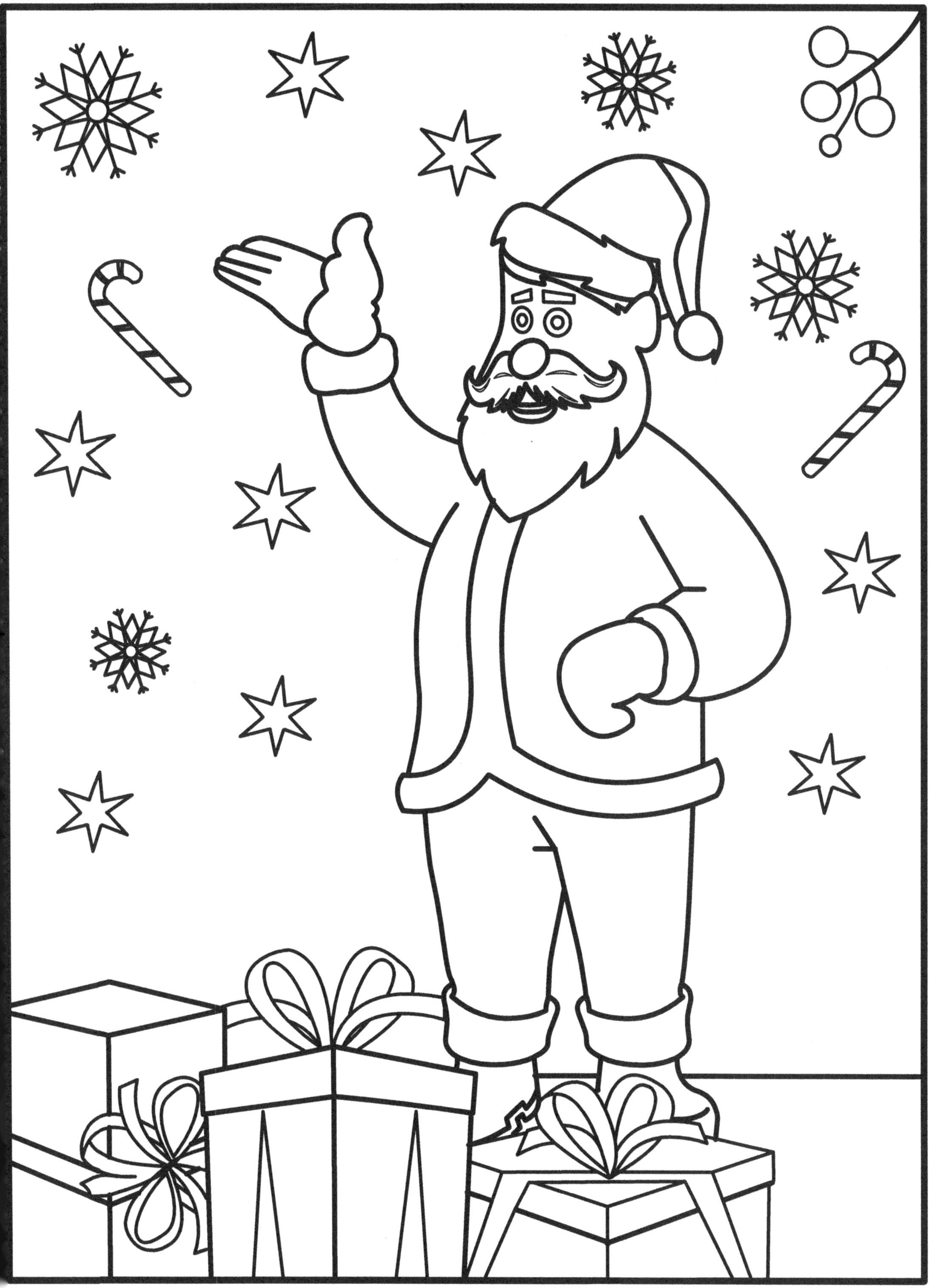

Made in the USA
Las Vegas, NV
02 December 2022

60981366R00037